Alfred's **INSTRUMENTAL** MP3 CD **PLAY-ALONG**

Ultimate Movie
Instrumental Solos

Arranged by Bill Galliford, Ethan Neuburg, and Tod Edmondson
Recordings produced by Dan Warner, Doug Emery, Lee Levin and Artemis Music Limited.

© 2012 Alfred Music Publishing Co., Inc.
All Rights Reserved. Printed in USA.

ISBN-10: 0-7390-9190-5
ISBN-13: 978-0-7390-9190-6

Alfred

♻ **Alfred Cares.** Contents printed on 100% recycled paper.

CONTENTS

mp3 CD Track — Demo — Play-Along

AUGIE'S GREAT MUNICIPAL BAND

(from *Star Wars Episode I: The Phantom Menace*)

Track 2: Demo
Track 3: Play-Along

Music by
JOHN WILLIAMS

ACROSS THE STARS

(Love Theme from *Star Wars Episode II: Attack of the Clones*)

Track 4: Demo
Track 5: Play-Along

Music by
JOHN WILLIAMS

Across the Stars - 2 - 1

ANAKIN'S THEME
(from *Star Wars Episode I: The Phantom Menace*)

Track 6: Demo
Track 7: Play-Along

Music by
JOHN WILLIAMS

Moderato (♩ = 76)

Anakin's Theme - 2 - 1

BATTLE OF THE HEROES

(from *Star Wars Episode III: Revenge of the Sith*)

Track 8: Demo
Track 9: Play-Along

Music by
JOHN WILLIAMS

Maestoso, with great force (♩ = 92)

Battle of the Heroes - 2 - 1

9

CAN YOU READ MY MIND?

(Love Theme from *Superman*)

Words by LESLIE BRICUSSE
Music by JOHN WILLIAMS

Track 10: Demo
Track 11: Play-Along

CONCERNING HOBBITS

(from The Lord of the Rings: The Fellowship of the Ring)

Track 12: Demo
Track 13: Play-Along

Music by
HOWARD SHORE

Moderately (♩ = 104)

Track 14: Demo
Track 15: Play-Along

CANTINA BAND

(from *Star Wars Episode IV: A New Hope*)

Music by
JOHN WILLIAMS

Moderately fast ragtime (♩ = 112)

To Coda ⊕

Cantina Band - 2 - 1

DIAMONDS ARE FOREVER

Track 16: Demo
Track 17: Play-Along

Music by JOHN BARRY
Lyric by DON BLACK

Moderately (♩ = 104)

Track 18: Demo
Track 19: Play-Along

DOUBLE TROUBLE
(from *Harry Potter and the Prisoner of Azkaban*)

Music by
JOHN WILLIAMS

Medieval in spirit (♩ = 92)

DING-DONG! THE WITCH IS DEAD

(from *The Wizard of Oz*)

Track 20: Demo
Track 21: Play-Along

Music by HAROLD ARLEN
Lyric by E.Y. HARBURG

Moderately bright march (♩ = 116)

Ding-Dong! The Witch Is Dead - 2 - 1

17

Ding-Dong! The Witch Is Dead - 2 - 2

DUEL OF THE FATES

(from *Star Wars Episode I: The Phantom Menace*)

Track 22: Demo
Track 23: Play-Along

Music by
JOHN WILLIAMS

Duel of the Fates - 2 - 1

EVENSTAR

(from *The Lord of the Rings: The Two Towers*)

Music by HOWARD SHORE
Text by J.R.R. TOLKIEN

Track 24: Demo
Track 25: Play-Along

FOLLOW THE YELLOW BRICK ROAD/ WE'RE OFF TO SEE THE WIZARD

(from *The Wizard of Oz*)

Track 26: Demo
Track 27: Play-Along

Music by HAROLD ARLEN
Lyric by E.Y. HARBURG

Moderate march (♩. = 128)

FAMILY PORTRAIT
(from *Harry Potter and the Sorcerer's Stone*)

Track 28: Demo
Track 29: Play-Along

Music by
JOHN WILLIAMS

Slowly, with expression (♩ = 80)

* An easier 8th-note alternative figure has been provided.

Family Portrait - 2 - 1

*E♯ = F
**A♯ = B♭

FAWKES THE PHOENIX

(from *Harry Potter and the Chamber of Secrets*)

Track 30: Demo
Track 31: Play-Along

Music by
JOHN WILLIAMS

Fawkes the Phoenix - 2 - 1

*An easier 8th-note alternative figure has been provided.

Fawkes the Phoenix - 2 - 2

FOR YOUR EYES ONLY

Track 32: Demo
Track 33: Play-Along

Music by BILL CONTI
Lyrics by MICHAEL LEESON

FROM RUSSIA WITH LOVE

Track 34: Demo
Track 35: Play-Along

Words and Music by
LIONEL BART

GOLDFINGER

Track 36: Demo
Track 37: Play-Along

Music by JOHN BARRY
Lyrics by LESLIE BRICUSSE
and ANTHONY NEWLEY

Moderately (♩ = 104)

HARRY'S WONDROUS WORLD

(from *Harry Potter and the Sorcerer's Stone*)

Track 38: Demo
Track 39: Play-Along

Music by
JOHN WILLIAMS

Harry's Wondrous World - 3 - 1

* E♯ = F

101 **Stately and nobly**
legato
mf

f
mf

117
f

rit.

a tempo
ff

GOLLUM'S SONG

(from *The Lord of the Rings: The Two Towers*)

Track 40: Demo
Track 41: Play-Along

Music by HOWARD SHORE
Words by FRAN WALSH

Moderately, flowing (♩ = 104)

Gollum's Song - 2 - 1

Gollum's Song - 2 - 2

GONNA FLY NOW

(Theme from *Rocky*)

Track 42: Demo
Track 43: Play-Along

Words and Music by
BILL CONTI, AYN ROBBINS
and CAROL CONNORS

Gonna Fly Now - 2 - 1

HEDWIG'S THEME
(from *Harry Potter and the Sorcerer's Stone*)

Track 44: Demo
Track 45: Play-Along

Music by
JOHN WILLIAMS

I SWEAR

(from *The Social Network*)

Words and Music by
GARY BAKER and FRANK MYERS

Moderately slow (♩ = 88)

IF I ONLY HAD A BRAIN

(from *The Wizard of Oz*)

Track 48: Demo
Track 49: Play-Along

Music by HAROLD ARLEN
Lyric by E.Y. HARBURG

IN DREAMS

(from *The Lord of the Rings: The Fellowship of the Ring*)

Track 50: Demo
Track 51: Play-Along

Words and Music by
FRAN WALSH and
HOWARD SHORE

Moderately slow (♩ = 76)

JAMES BOND THEME

(from *Dr. No*)

By
MONTY NORMAN

Track 52: Demo
Track 53: Play-Along

Moderately bright (♩ = 138)

LEAVING HOGWARTS
(from *Harry Potter and the Sorcerer's Stone*)

Music by
JOHN WILLIAMS

Track 54: Demo
Track 55: Play-Along

Track 56: Demo
Track 57: Play-Along

LILY'S THEME

(Main Theme from *Harry Potter and the Deathly Hallows, Part 2*)

Music by
ALEXANDRE DESPLAT

MANY MEETINGS

(from *The Lord of the Rings: The Fellowship of the Ring*)

Music by
HOWARD SHORE

Track 58: Demo
Track 59: Play-Along

LIVE AND LET DIE

Words and Music by
PAUL McCARTNEY and
LINDA McCARTNEY

Track 60: Demo
Track 61: Play-Along

Live and Let Die - 2 - 1

MARION'S THEME

(from *Raiders of the Lost Ark*)

Music by
JOHN WILLIAMS

MAY THE FORCE BE WITH YOU
(from *Star Wars Episode IV: A New Hope*)

Track 64: Demo
Track 65: Play-Along

Music by
JOHN WILLIAMS

NOBODY DOES IT BETTER

(from *The Spy Who Loved Me*)

Track 66: Demo
Track 67: Play-Along

Music by MARVIN HAMLISCH
Lyrics by CAROLE BAYER SAGER

OBLIVIATE
(from *Harry Potter and the Deathly Hallows, Part 2*)

Track 68: Demo
Track 69: Play-Along

Music by
ALEXANDRE DESPLAT

Track 70: Demo
Track 71: Play-Along

ON HER MAJESTY'S
SECRET SERVICE

By JOHN BARRY

Maestoso (♩ = 120)

(You're Out of the Woods)
OPTIMISTIC VOICES
(from The Wizard of Oz)

Lyric by
E.Y. HARBURG

Music by
HAROLD ARLEN and
HERBERT STOTHART

Track 74: Demo
Track 75: Play-Along

OVER THE RAINBOW

(from *The Wizard of Oz*)

Lyric by
E.Y. HARBURG

Music by
HAROLD ARLEN

Slowly, with expression (♩ = 88)

PRINCESS LEIA'S THEME

(from *Star Wars Episode IV: A New Hope*)

Track 76: Demo
Track 77: Play-Along

Music by
JOHN WILLIAMS

Moderately slow, with a gentle flow (♩ = 72)

RAIDERS MARCH

(from *Raiders of the Lost Ark*)

Music by
JOHN WILLIAMS

Raiders March - 2 - 1

Track 80: Demo
Track 81: Play-Along

ROHAN
(from *The Lord of the Rings: The Two Towers*)

Text by
J.R.R. TOLKIEN

Music by
HOWARD SHORE

SONG FROM M*A*S*H

(Suicide Is Painless)

Track 82: Demo
Track 83: Play-Along

Words and Music by
MIKE ALTMAN and JOHNNY MANDEL

STAR WARS
(Main Theme)
(from *Star Wars Episode IV: A New Hope*

Track 84: Demo
Track 85: Play-Along

Music by
JOHN WILLIAMS

STATUES
(from *Harry Potter and the Deathly Hallows, Part 2*)

By
ALEXANDRE DESPLAT

Moderately, with movement (♩ = 132)

THE STEWARD OF GONDOR

(from *The Lord of the Rings: The Return of the King*)

Track 88: Demo
Track 89: Play-Along

Lyrics by
J.R.R. TOLKIEN
Adapted by
PHILIPPA BOYENS

Music by
HOWARD SHORE
Contains the Composition "The Edge Of Night"
Melody by BILLY BOYD

Track 90: Demo
Track 91: Play-Along

THE BLACK RIDER
(from *The Lord of the Rings: The Fellowship of the Ring*)

Music by
HOWARD SHORE

THEME FROM SUPERMAN

Track 92: Demo
Track 93: Play-Along

Music by
JOHN WILLIAMS

Theme from Superman - 2 - 1

THE ARENA
(from *Star Wars Episode II: Attack of the Clones*)

Music by
JOHN WILLIAMS

The Arena - 2 - 1

THE IMPERIAL MARCH
(DARTH VADER'S THEME)

(from *Star Wars Episode V: The Empire Strikes Back*)

Track 96: Demo
Track 97: Play-Along

Music by
JOHN WILLIAMS

March style (♩ = 108)

(Tempo click)

THE LULLABY LEAGUE/
THE LOLLIPOP GUILD/
WE WELCOME YOU TO MUNCHKINLAND

(from The Wizard of Oz)

Track 98: Demo
Track 99: Play-Along

Music by HAROLD ARLEN
Lyric by E.Y. HARBURG

Moderately fast (♩ = 144)

3 *"The Lullaby League/The Lollipop Guild"*

mp

1. **2.**

mf

14 *"We Welcome You to Munchkinland"*

2

28

molto rit.

THE MEADOW PICNIC

(from *Star Wars Episode II: Attack of the Clones*)

Track 100: Demo
Track 101: Play-Along

Music by
JOHN WILLIAMS

THE MERRY OLD LAND OF OZ
(from *The Wizard of Oz*)

Track 102: Demo
Track 103: Play-Along

Music by HAROLD ARLEN
Lyric by E.Y. HARBURG

THE NOTEBOOK
(Main Title)

Track 104: Demo
Track 105: Play-Along

Written by
AARON ZIGMAN

Slowly, with expression (♩ = 69)

THE PROPHECY

(from *The Lord of the Rings: The Fellowship of the Ring*)

Track 106: Demo
Track 107: Play-Along

Music by HOWARD SHORE
Text by J.R.R. TOLKIEN
Adapted by PHILLIPPA BOYENS

THE PINK PANTHER

(from *The Pink Panther*)

Track 108: Demo
Track 109: Play-Along

By HENRY MANCINI

Moderately, mysterious (♩ = 120)

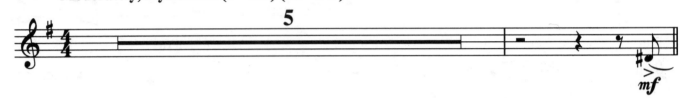

The Pink Panther - 2 - 1

THE THRONE ROOM

(from *Star Wars Episode IV: A New Hope*)

Track 110: Demo
Track 111: Play-Along

Music by
JOHN WILLIAMS

Maestoso (♩ = 112)
(*Tempo Click*)

f marc.

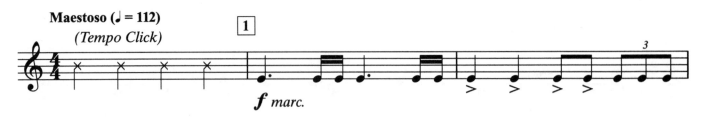

The Throne Room - 2 - 1

THUNDERBALL
(Main Theme)

Track 112: Demo
Track 113: Play-Along

Music by JOHN BARRY
Lyric by DON BLACK

Moderately slow (♩ = 92)

TOMORROW NEVER DIES

Track 114: Demo
Track 115: Play-Along

Words and Music by
SHERYL CROW and
MITCHELL FROOM

WIZARD WHEEZES
(from *Harry Potter and the Half-Blood Prince*)

Track 116: Demo
Track 117: Play-Along

Music by
NICHOLAS HOOPER

Up-tempo big band swing (♩ = 208) (♫ = ♪³♪)

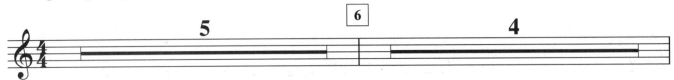

Wizard Wheezes - 2 - 1

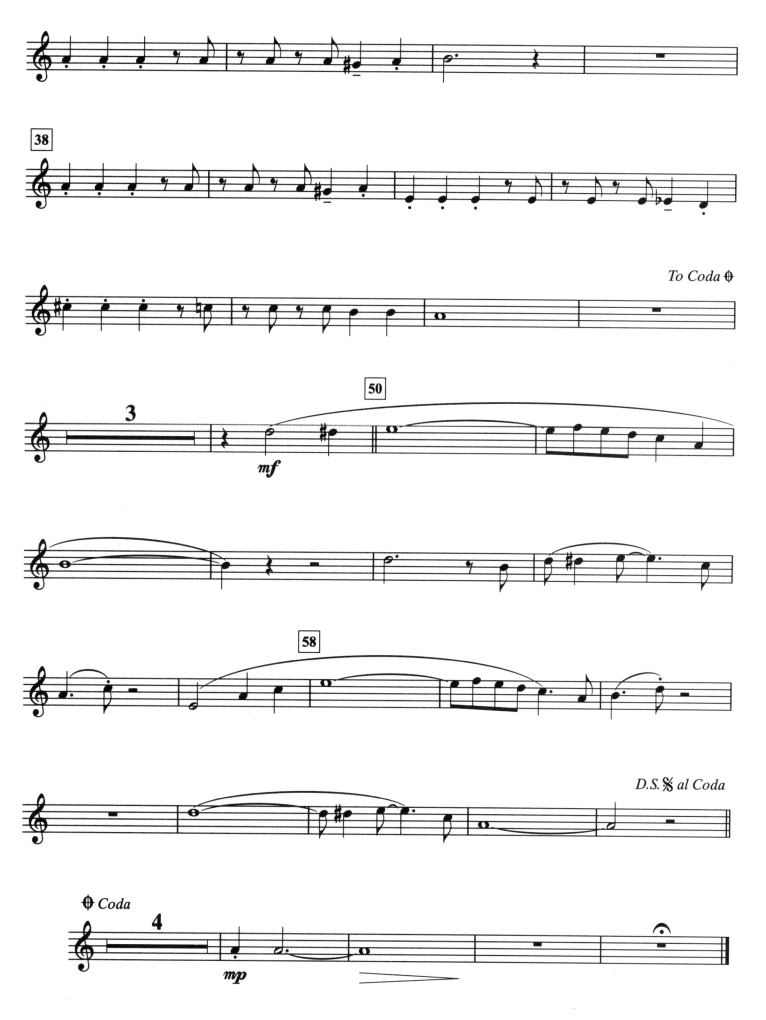

WONKA'S WELCOME SONG
(from *Charlie and the Chocolate Factory*)

Track 118: Demo
Track 119: Play-Along

Words by JOHN AUGUST and DANNY ELFMAN
Music by DANNY ELFMAN

Bright two-beat style (♩ = 120)

(À la yodel)

YOU ONLY LIVE TWICE

Track 120: Demo
Track 121: Play-Along

Music by JOHN BARRY
Lyric by LESLIE BRICUSSE

PARTS OF A TENOR SAXOPHONE
AND FINGERING CHART

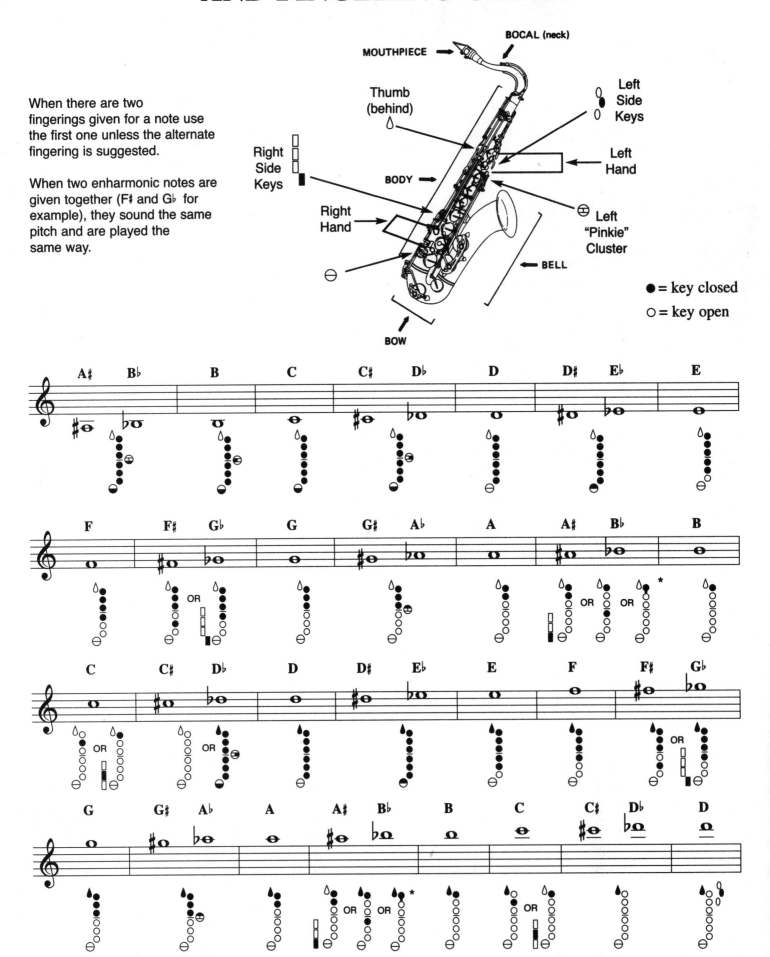

When there are two fingerings given for a note use the first one unless the alternate fingering is suggested.

When two enharmonic notes are given together (F♯ and G♭ for example), they sound the same pitch and are played the same way.

MOUTHPIECE

BOCAL (neck)

Thumb (behind)

Left Side Keys

Right Side Keys

Left Hand

BODY

Left "Pinkie" Cluster

Right Hand

BELL

BOW

● = key closed
○ = key open

* Both pearl keys are pressed with left hand 1st finger.

INSTRUMENTAL SOLOS

This instrumental series contains themes from Blizzard Entertainment's popular massively multiplayer online role-playing game and includes 4 pages of art from the World of Warcraft universe. The compatible arrangements are carefully edited for the Level 2–3 player, and include an accompaniment CD which features a demo track and play-along track. Titles: Lion's Pride • The Shaping of the World • Pig and Whistle • Slaughtered Lamb • Invincible • A Call to Arms • Gates of the Black Temple • Salty Sailor • Wrath of the Lich King • Garden of Life.

(00-36626) I Flute Book & CD I $12.99

(00-36629) I Clarinet Book & CD I $12.99

(00-36632) I Alto Sax Book & CD I $12.99

(00-36635) I Tenor Sax Book & CD I $12.99

(00-36638) I Trumpet Book & CD I $12.99

(00-36641) I Horn in F Book & CD I $12.99

(00-36644) I Trombone Book & CD I $12.99

(00-36647) I Piano Acc. Book & CD I $14.99

(00-36650) I Violin Book & CD I $16.99

(00-36653) I Viola Book & CD I $16.99

(00-36656) I Cello Book & CD I $16.99

LICENSED BLIZZARD ENTERTAINMENT PRODUCT

Harry Potter
INSTRUMENTAL SOLOS

Play-along with the best-known themes from the Harry Potter film series! The compatible arrangements are carefully edited for the Level 2–3 player, and include an accompaniment CD which features a demo track and play-along track.

Titles: Double Trouble • Family Portrait • Farewell to Dobby • Fawkes the Phoenix • Fireworks • Harry in Winter • Harry's Wondrous World • Hedwig's Theme • Hogwarts' Hymn • Hogwarts' March • Leaving Hogwarts • Lily's Theme • Obliviate • Statues • A Window to the Past • Wizard Wheezes.

(00-39211) | Flute Book & CD | $12.99

(00-39214) | Clarinet Book & CD | $12.99

(00-39217) | Alto Sax Book & CD | $12.99

(00-39220) | Tenor Sax Book & CD | $12.99

(00-39223) | Trumpet Book & CD | $12.99

(00-39226) | Horn in F Book & CD | $12.99

(00-39229) | Trombone Book & CD | $12.99

(00-39232) | Piano Acc. Book & CD | $18.99

(00-39235) | Violin Book & CD | $18.99

(00-39238) | Viola Book & CD | $18.99

(00-39241) | Cello Book & CD | $18.99